T0274902

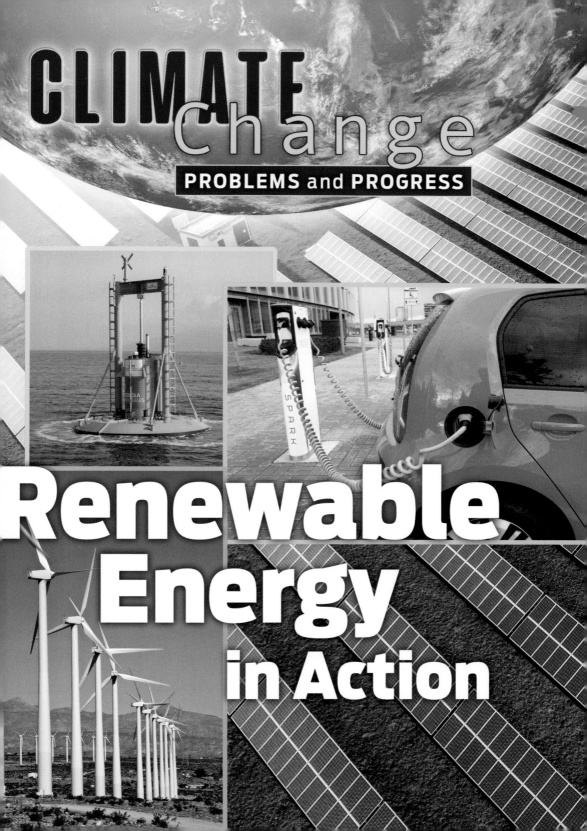

CLIMATE Change

PROBLEMS and PROGRESS

Renewable Energy
in Action

CLIMATE Change

PROBLEMS and PROGRESS

Renewable
Energy in Action

James Shoals

Mason Crest

Mason Crest
450 Parkway Drive, Suite D
Broomall, PA 19008
www.masoncrest.com

© 2020 by Mason Crest, an imprint of National Highlights, Inc.

Printed and bound in the United States of America.

Series ISBN: 978-1-4222-4353-4
Hardback ISBN: 978-1-4222-4359-6
EBook ISBN: 978-1-4222-7454-5

First printing
1 3 5 7 9 8 6 4 2

Cover photographs by Dreamstime: Timrobertsaerial (bottom); Toxawww (right); Vallo84sl (bkgd).

Library of Congress Cataloging-in-Publication Data is on file with the publisher.

QR Codes disclaimer:

CONTENTS

KEY ICONS TO LOOK FOR

Words to Understand: These words with their easy-to-understand definitions will increase the reader's understanding of the text, while building vocabulary skills.

Sidebars: This boxed material within the main text allows readers to build knowledge, gain insights, explore possibilities, and broaden their perspectives by weaving together additional information to provide realistic and holistic perspectives.

Educational Videos: Readers can view videos by scanning our QR codes, providing them with additional educational content to supplement the text. Examples include news coverage, moments in history, speeches, iconic moments, and much more!

Text-Dependent Questions: These questions send the reader back to the text for more careful attention to the evidence presented here.

Research Projects: Readers are pointed toward areas of further inquiry connected to each chapter. Suggestions are provided for projects that encourage deeper research and analysis.

Series Glossary of Key Terms: This back-of-the-book glossary contains terminology used through-out this series. Words found here increase the reader's ability to read and comprehend higher-level books and articles in this field.

automate a process where machines do work to save human effort

biomass the plant and animal substances used for fuel

boon something that brings great benefits

coastal near the land beside a sea

concentration the amount of a substance present in something

conventional something which is usual or traditional

decompose to slowly and naturally decay

drill to make a hole in something

drought a long period of time when there is little or no rain, and crops die

efficient something that works well and produces good results by using the available energy in an effective way

emission the act of releasing gas or heat into air

generating capacity the amount of power which a power plant can produce at a time

harness to bring under control for effective use

hurdle a barrier or an obstacle

hurricane a severe cyclone with a wind speed more than 70 miles per hour, accompanied by heavy rain and lightning

Industrial Revolution a period from the late 1700s to the early 1800s when machines were used for doing work

insulate to cover with a material that prevents leakage or the transfer of heat

irreversible impossible to change

mechanical operated by a system of machines

offshore in the sea; not on land

precipitation rain, snow, or hail

replenish to bring something back to its previous levels by filling it up again

reverse to turn to an opposite situation

turbine a machine with blades rotated by the pressure of steam, air, or water

INTRODUCTION

lobal warming is causing extreme climatic changes, such as the melting of glaciers, droughts, heatwaves, untimely precipitation, and shifting of the seasons. The blanket of greenhouse gases (GHGs) around the Earth is growing thicker and denser every day, giving more warmth to the Earth than required. The burning of fossil fuels to obtain energy is the main contributor to GHGs. The threat of global warming may become extremely serious if the current trend continues. Moreover, fossil fuels are nonrenewable resources, which will be exhausted in the future.

Therefore, we need to conserve our fossil fuels. To achieve that, we will have to look for alternative sources of energy that can be renewed. Renewable sources are replenished by nature. Sun, wind, water, and the heat inside the Earth have tremendous potential for energy production and can easily substitute fossil fuels. Unlike fossil fuels, however, they do not release harmful emissions and are environment-friendly. Reducing and recycling solid waste is an active way to reduce GHG emissions. It saves waste from ending up in landfills where it produces GHGs. The manufacture, distribution, and use of products as well as management of the resulting waste lead to GHG emissions.

Fossil Fuels

Fossil fuels are created from fossilized plants and animals. Millions of years ago, our Earth was covered with swamps and bogs. There were a variety of plants and animals around. After these plants and animals died, they were buried under layers of mud, sand, and silt. Over the years, the dead plants and animals decomposed into organic materials to form fossil fuels.

Source of World's Energy

More than 90 percent of our energy demands are met by fossil fuels. One of their main uses is to generate electricity—an essential requirement of our daily life. They are also used to power vehicles, heat homes, and run industries.

Main Fossil Fuels

Coal, oil, and natural gas are the main fossil fuels. Coal is an easily combustible brownish-black rock that is present in layers below the surface of Earth called coal beds. Crude oil is smelly and yellow or black in color. It is usually found in underground areas called reservoirs. Natural gas is a mixture of certain gases with the highest percentage of methane.

Biggest Contributor to Warming

The biggest problem with the use of fossil fuels is the **irreversible** environmental damage they cause. Burning coal, oil, and natural gas releases billions of tons of carbon dioxide (CO_2) and other harmful GHGs into the atmosphere. This is the primary cause of damage to the ozone layer and of global warming.

PETROLEUM AND NATURAL GAS FORMATION

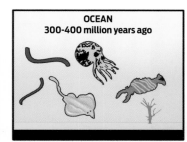

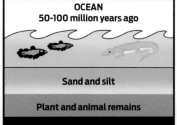

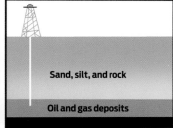

Tiny sea plants and animals died and were buried in the ocean floor. Over time, they were covered by layers of silt and sand.

Over millions of years, the remains were buried deeper and deeper. Enormous heat and pressure turned them into oil and gas.

Today, we drill down through layers of sand, silt, and rock to reach the rock formation that contains oil and gas deposits.

Climate Facts

- Coal accounts for nearly half of all the resources used in the generation of electricity.

- According to scientists, our current oil and natural gas reserves will be depleted after fifty years, while those of coal will last for another 150 to 200 years.

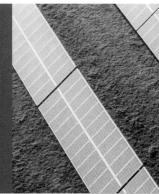

Future Energy Needs

Currently, about 80–85 percent of the world's energy comes from fossil fuels. Renewable energy sources provide only the remaining 15–20 percent of the required energy. Since the demand for energy is growing, the use of fossil fuels to produce energy is bound to increase. The use of fossil fuels will further increase global warming as they release large volumes of CO_2.

Future Projections

According to the Intergovernmental Panel on Climate Change (IPCC), an international organization set up by the World Meteorological Organization (WMO), the global temperature might rise from 6.1 to 11°F (3.4 to 6.1°C) during the twenty-first century if people continue exploiting fossil fuels at a high rate. Sea levels are expected to rise by 7 to 23 inches (18 to 59 cm). Natural calamities like **hurricanes**, storms, floods, and **droughts** will become frequent. Due to the melting of ice caps, the availability of fresh water will reduce, thus creating a shortage of drinking water. Many species of plants and animals would become extinct.

Future Energy Needs

The world population continues to rise, and so do the energy needs. The total industrial use of energy is likely to grow to around 28 percent by 2040. By the same year, residential and commercial energy demands are expected to rise by about 30 percent. The transportation demands of various industries will increase about 45 percent. With energy demands increasing at a rapid pace, there is a pressing need to develop some alternative sources to produce energy.

Climate Facts

- Through the first half of the twentieth century, global warming was thought to be good for countries with very low temperatures.

- Since the Industrial Revolution, the concentrations of CO_2 and methane in the atmosphere have increased by 40 percent and 148 percent respectively.

Solar Energy

ince ancient times humans have used solar energy in multiple ways. However, as world civilizations grew, fossil fuels were discovered and people gradually moved away from solar energy. For the past few decades, people have realized the scarcity of fossil fuels as well as their harmful effects. Once again, they are trying to harness and use solar energy.

Solar Solution

Solar energy can be converted into electricity without burning fossil fuels. According to the European Photovoltaic Industry Association, solar power can be used to meet more than one-fourth of the world's energy requirements by 2040. Solar energy can also replace fossil fuels in cooking, heating water, and space heating.

Solar Thermal Power Plants

Solar power plants produce electricity from solar energy. They use mirrors and lenses to focus a large area of sunlight into a small beam and achieve higher temperatures. The heat produced is then used to boil water and drive a steam turbine that generates electricity without creating any harmful emissions.

Photovoltaic Cells

Solar panels made of photovoltaic cells (PV) are a popular technology used to convert solar energy into electricity. Photovoltaic cells are made of semiconductor materials like silicon. When sunlight hits these cells, it frees electrons from their atoms. The flow of electrons through the cell generates electricity.

Climate Facts

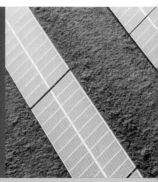

• Kamuthi Solar Power Project in the Indian state of Tamil Nadu is the largest solar energy-generating facility in the world. It powers one hundred fifty thousand homes.

• The photovoltaic effect was discovered by a French physicist, A. E Becquerel, in 1954.

Solar-powered Objects

f we were to use less than 0.02 percent of the available solar energy, we could easily replace fossil fuels and nuclear power as energy sources. Though small devices such as solar cookers and solar calculators are already in use, bigger technologies such as solar cars are still a future dream.

Solar Lamps

Solar lamps are connected with solar panels that not only provide light to the lamps, but can also be used to charge mobile phones. They are a boon for people who do not have access to electricity. Solar cells can also be used to light solar lamps.

Solar Cars

Solar cars are still in the developmental stages. Long, wide, and flat, they look like a tabletop on wheels. Emissions from automobiles worldwide are the second biggest cause of global warming. The use of solar cars, which run on electricity produced by their solar panels, can help in reducing global warming. They do not emit CO_2 like other vehicles.

Solar Cookers

Solar cookers make use of direct sunlight for heating or cooking food. These low-tech devices are also priced reasonably. Since they use no fuel, they are a very practical option for reducing fuel wastage. Solar cookers are becoming increasingly popular with the growing awareness of the need to conserve fossil fuels.

Solar cars in action

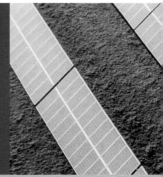

Climate Facts

- In 1990, a solar-powered aircraft flew 2,552 miles (4,060 km) across the United States, setting a world record.

- The first satellite to use solar panels was Vanguard 1. It was launched by the United States in 1958.

Passive Solar Energy

Solar energy can be used without any **mechanical** or electric device for providing heat and daylight to a house or a building. This solar heat is known as passive solar energy. The design of a building plays a crucial role in determining its ability to tap solar energy.

Passive Solar Heating

Buildings can be designed to absorb maximum heat from the sun with the help of appropriately placed windows, and heat-absorbing floors and walls. Once heat has entered a building, its well-**insulated** and airtight design can prevent heat from escaping. According to the New Mexico Solar Energy Association, depending on the climate and design, almost 100 percent of a building's heating needs can be met with solar energy.

Passive Solar Building Design

Conventional houses are poorly designed—they do not have the advantage of tapping natural light. We can fight global warming by building energy-**efficient** homes, which capture solar energy naturally for heating a house in the winters and cooling it in the summers. Such homes help reduce our dependence on fossil fuels by minimizing the need for electricity-based heating or cooling devices.

Passive Cooling

The design of a building can also help in keeping a house cool during the summers, thus reducing the need for air-conditioning. Techniques such as reducing the window size and using reflective materials in external walls and roof are used for passive cooling. Shading devices like eves or vegetation keep solar radiation away.

Climate Facts

• External shading devices can reduce the heat gains of a building by 90 percent.

• Passive solar building designs can bring down the heating bills of a house by 50 percent.

Solar Heating in Homes

Though our homes do not emit pollutants, they still contribute to global warming. The electricity used in our homes comes from power plants that burn fossil fuels to produce power. We can do our bit in fighting global warming by avoiding the overuse of fossil fuels and using devices such as solar water heaters, solar ovens, and others.

Solar Water Heaters

Currently, solar water heating systems heat water for more than seventy million households worldwide. In countries with extremely low temperatures, where a lot of power is spent heating household water, solar water heaters can greatly reduce the dependence on fossil fuels.

Solar Pool Heaters

A solar pool heater can be used for heating water in a swimming pool. The pool water is circulated through solar panels where it gets heated by the sun. It is then returned to the pool. A solar pool heater can displace between five and ten tons of GHGs annually.

Solar Space Heating Systems

Space heating refers to the internal heating of the space inside a building. Solar collectors placed on the rooftops collect the thermal energy of the sun, which is used to heat the space inside a building. These use either a solid or a liquid base to absorb solar energy and distribute it through pumps, fans, and blowers.

How does solar water heating work?

Climate Facts

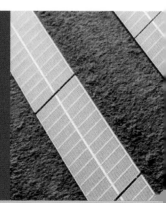

• Solar water heaters in North Carolina bring down its global warming pollution, equivalent to taking 300,000 cars off the road.

• A solar oven can be made at home by surrounding a cardboard box with layers of insulation and aluminum wrapping.

Solar Energy in Space

The sun is a reliable source of a tremendous amount of energy. Ever since the world has woken up to the threat posed by global warming, efforts are being made to tap the sun's energy and channel it to meet our daily needs. Researchers around the world are now trying to find ways to tap solar energy in space and use it on Earth.

Advantages

The level of solar irradiance is about 1.4 times in space than at the Earth's surface. In solar power plants on Earth, the panels can collect solar power for only six to eight hours a day, whereas in a space-based power plant, solar power can be collected throughout the day. Also, energy collection in space is not influenced by changes in weather or the time of the day, as it is on Earth.

Transportation

In areas like the Sahara Desert, huge amounts of quality solar energy can be collected, but it cannot be used due to problems in transportation to the areas that need it the most. The idea of using space-based solar power is driven by the need to target areas that are difficult to reach. Scientists plan to use microwaves or lasers to beam the energy collected in space back to specific areas on Earth. This would reduce the need to store on the ground the energy derived from renewable sources.

Climate Facts

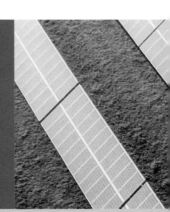

- Scientists claim that they have the technology to put a large structure in space that could gather enough energy to power a large city.

- Dezhou, China, can be called a "solar city" as most of its population uses solar hot water systems and solar electricity.

Wind Energy

The use of wind energy for generating power is not a recent discovery. A few centuries ago, humans realized the tremendous potential of wind as a source of energy. However, we still need to find more ways to tap wind energy and use it effectively to bring down global warming.

Wind Power for Electricity

Wind power currently supplies about 3.7 percent of the electricity of the world, and is growing at an annual rate of almost 36 percent. As of 2012, one hundred countries around the world are using wind energy to produce electricity. Nearly 42.1 percent of the electricity in Denmark, 24 percent in Portugal, 20.2 percent in Spain, 21.1 percent in Ireland and 13.3 percent in Germany is produced using wind energy. It has lowered their consumption of fossil fuels, thus bringing down the **emission** of GHGs.

Wind Turbines

Over time, windmills used for generating electricity came to be known as wind turbines. Wind **turbines** can be as tall as a twenty-story building, and can have long blades. The force of winds spins the blades of the turbine, and the energy of this motion is converted into electricity through a generator.

Early Uses

Our ancestors used wind energy for grinding grain and pumping underground water. Between the eighteenth and nineteenth centuries, humans discovered that wind power could be used to generate electricity. The first windmill used for producing electricity was built in Scotland in July 1887 by Professor James Blyth. He used it for lighting his cottage.

How wind turbines work

Climate Facts

- Currently, China has the greatest wind power production capacity, with 168,700 Mw (megawatts) in operation.

- Almost one-fifth of Denmark's electricity is produced by wind turbines.

Wind Farms

Wind farms are places where tens and sometimes hundreds of wind turbines are built together to generate electricity. They are a **boon** for the environment as they produce electricity in a clean, nonpolluting manner.

The Hurdle of Location

The main **hurdle** in **harnessing** wind energy is its irregular nature. Some areas on Earth experience strong and continuous winds. **Coastal** areas, hilltops, and open plains are some of the best locations for building wind farms.

Floating Wind Turbines

Floating farms are a relatively new concept developed in the mid-1990s. While offshore wind farms can be constructed only to a depth of 130 feet (40 m) in water, floating farms float in waters as deep as 2,300 feet (700 m). They take advantage of the fastest blowing winds in the middle of the ocean.

Offshore Wind Farms

Some turbines are built on waterbodies. They are mounted to the floor through a long tower. They are more efficient in harnessing wind power than those on land, as winds blow at much greater speeds over bodies of water. Offshore wind turbine technology has developed at a fast pace in the last few years.

Climate Facts

• The Gansu Wind Farm in China is the largest wind farm located on land, with a capacity of generating 20,000 Mw of power by 2020.

• A study has shown that almost 70 percent of the electricity required by the United States can be met with offshore wind power within 50 miles (80 km) of the US coastline.

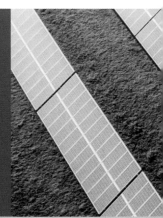

Geothermal Energy

eothermal energy refers to the heat generated and stored within the Earth. Some areas have a higher **concentration** of geothermal energy. The most active geothermal resources are found in areas with the highest underground temperatures. Sometimes geothermal energy finds its way to the surface of the Earth in the form of volcanoes and hot springs.

Geothermal Heat Pumps

Since ancient times, water from hot springs has been used for bathing, cooking, and heating. One of the most common uses of geothermal energy is heating or cooling a building using geothermal heat pumps, also known as ground source heat pumps (GSHP). Geothermal heat pumps transfer heat from the ground or water into buildings in the winter. In the summer, this process is **reversed**.

Geothermal Power Plants

Dry steam plants, flash steam plants, and binary cycle power plants are the three types of geothermal power plants. Geothermal power plants obtain their fuel—dry steam or hot water—from deep below the Earth's surface. This is done by **drilling** wells into the earth and piping dry steam or hot water to the surface, which are then used to turn the generator turbines and produce electricity.

Geothermal energy in Iceland

Climate Facts

- The first geothermal power plant of the world was built at Larderello, Italy, in 1911.

- At present, geothermal energy is used worldwide to generate electricity in twenty-four countries and for heating purposes in seventy countries.

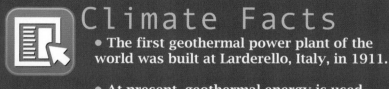

Geothermal Energy in the Future

Many governments are trying to encourage the use of geothermal energy as an alternative for the future. The US government offers financial assistance to organizations that choose geothermal energy resources over fossil fuels. Those that are still largely dependent on fossil fuels have to pay a higher cost for doing so.

Economic Boost

In the United States—the world leader in producing electricity from geothermal energy—about 3,591 Mw of energy per year is produced using geothermal sources. This accounts for $1 billion of revenue. Indonesia is another country with a tremendous potential to produce 29,215 Mw of geothermal energy per year. This will account for $7.3 billion of revenue each year.

A Future Alternative?

The cost of producing energy from geothermal sources is declining. This makes it a viable option for the future. Some geothermal facilities have reduced the price of electricity by 50 percent since 1980. The direct use of geothermal resources as a source of heating and cooling of homes also has a bright future. Further developments in the technology to harness geothermal energy will make it a more useful future alternative.

Iceland: A Unique Example

The high concentration of volcanoes in Iceland makes it rich in geothermal energy. Nearly 90 percent of the homes in Iceland are heated by geothermal energy. Nearly 27 percent of the country's electricity is produced by its six geothermal power plants and the remaining comes mostly from hydropower.

Climate Facts

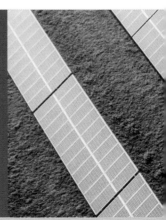

- Ninety percent of the world's geothermal plants are found along the "ring of fire," a horseshoe-shaped zone which circles the Pacific Ocean.

- Blue Lagoon, a hot water pond in Iceland formed by the salty wastewater from a geothermal power plant, is used by people for swimming and bathing.

Marine Energy

Marine energy, also known as ocean energy, has a tremendous potential to generate electricity to power our homes and industries. The movement of water in the oceans produces kinetic energy—energy in motion. There are four main sources of marine energy: tidal energy, wave energy, ocean thermal energy, and osmotic energy.

Power of Oceans

According to scientists, ocean energy has the potential to deliver ten million terawatt-hours of electricity per year. The clean and nonpolluting energy of oceans, once fully developed, can help to control global warming to a great extent.

Tidal Power

Tidal energy has been in use since the eleventh century. A large increase between low tide and high tide can be used to create energy. There are two different means to harness tidal energy. The first is to exploit the rise and fall of sea levels using dams or barrages, and the second is to harness tidal currents (the energy of moving water) using a marine turbine.

Ocean Thermal Energy

The sun's heat warms the surface water of oceans more than the deep ocean water. This temperature difference creates thermal energy, which can be used to run heat engines and produce electricity. This technology is presently being tested and developed by many countries. It is estimated that ocean thermal energy has the potential to generate several thousand terawatt-hours of electric power every year.

Tidal power generation

Climate Facts

● The Sihwa Lake Tidal Power Station of South Korea, with a power-generating capacity of 254 Mw, is the largest tidal power plant in the world.

● The Rance Tidal Power Station in France is the world's first tidal power station. It is also the second largest in the world.

Marine Energy (cont.)

At present, the use of ocean energy is very limited. Only a few small plants are found across the world, but it has captured the interest of scientists due to its huge potential to fight global warming. Scientists are now trying to develop technologies to tap marine energy in the best possible ways.

Wave Energy

In many areas of the world, the wind blows with enough force to produce continuous waves. The pressure fluctuations from below the surface are also responsible for causing waves. Ocean waves provide tremendous energy. The total power of waves hitting the world's coastlines is estimated to be two to three million mega-watts. Waves have enough energy to supply 10 percent of the world's electricity. However, harnessing this energy is difficult as waves carry enormous energy.

Harnessing Wave Energy

Both deep and shallow seawaters experience waves and are thus a potential source of wave power. Devices to capture wave energy have been designed to be installed on shorelines, offshore, and far offshore locations. Oscillating water column (OWC) is a shoreline device for capturing wave energy. Aqua Buoy and Wave Dragon are two common devices that harness energy from deepwater waves.

Osmotic Power

The mixing of freshwater and seawater at the point where a river flows into a salty ocean releases large amounts of energy that can be used for power production. This energy has very little impact on the environment. It is estimated that osmotic energy has the capacity of generating about 2,000 terawatt-hours of electricity every year.

Climate Facts

● Poseidon in Denmark is a floating power plant that produces both wave energy and wind energy. It is 37 m wide and 25 m long.

● Norway and Denmark are very active in the research and development of osmotic power.

Hydropower

T housands of years ago, the ancient Greeks, Romans, Arabs, Chinese, and Indians used waterwheels for grinding grains. Watermills powered by waterwheels were used to crush sugarcane to make sugar and to pound wood into pulp. During the nineteenth century, water turbines were developed to produce electricity.

Production of Hydroelectricity

The electricity generated using hydropower is known as hydroelectricity. To capture hydropower, huge concrete structures called dams are built on rivers. They block the flow of rivers and create vast reservoirs of water. The water released from a reservoir flows through a turbine and spins it. The spinning turbine in turn activates a generator, which produces electricity. Small hydropower plants use a canal to channel the river water through a turbine.

Hydropower Combats Global Warming

About one-fifth of the world's total electricity comes from hydropower plants. This is equivalent to releasing 20 percent less GHGs responsible for global warming than what would have been released, if the world's entire electricity was produced using fossil fuels. China, Brazil, Canada, and the United States are the largest producers of hydroelectric power worldwide. The Three Gorges Dam in China is the world's largest hydroelectric dam, with a capacity of generating 22,500 Mw of electricity.

Climate Facts

- The first hydroelectric power plant was built by Nikola Tesla and George Westinghouse in Niagara Falls.

- The Itaipu Power Plant in Brazil is the second largest power plant with a power-generating capacity of 14,000 Mw.

Hydropower (cont.)

Many countries have now realized the potential of hydropower. However, there has been a lot of debate on the viability of hydropower and its impact on the environment. It is a lesser-known fact that the generation of hydropower is also responsible for releasing methane, a GHG.

Positives

Hydropower is the cheapest renewable source for producing electricity. The only one-time cost required is the building of a dam. Water is constantly **replenished** on Earth by rainfall and snowfall. Moreover, the electricity production in dams is **automated** and hence does not involve any labor costs.

Pros and cons of hydropower

Drawbacks

Though dams and reservoirs do not burn any fuels, they can have a higher warming impact than even the dirtiest fossil fuel plants generating a similar quantity of electricity. Trees and plant matter settle to the bottom of a dam's reservoir when it is flooded. They **decompose** without oxygen and release huge quantities of methane. It is estimated that the large dams of the world together account for more than 4 percent of the global warming caused by human activities.

Solution

Scientists are planning to turn this drawback into a benefit by extracting methane from the reservoirs and using it as a fuel in thermoelectric plants to produce more electricity. A million tons of methane can generate about 1,760 Mw of electricity.

Climate Facts

- The United States has more than two thousand hydroelectric plants, which supply about 46 percent of its renewable electricity.

- Paraguay in South America produces nearly 100 percent of its electricity from hydroelectric dams.

Hydrogen Energy

Hydrogen is one of the primary elements of the universe. It can be used to generate power and heat with low or no emissions. Hydrogen can be obtained from compounds that contain it, such as fossil fuels, natural gas, and **biomass**. It can also be obtained from nuclear sources and renewable sources.

Types of Fuel Cells

Over the years, scientists have developed various types of fuel cells that have different applications. Polymer electrolyte membrane (PEM) is a type of fuel cell used to power automobiles and for stationary power production. Direct-methanol fuel cell (DMFC) can be used for powering portable electronic devices, such as laptop computers and battery rechargers. Other than PEM and DMFC, three more types of fuel cells are used in various applications: alkaline fuel cells, phosphoric acid fuel cells, and molten carbonate fuel cells.

Edge over Fossil Fuels

When fuel cells convert chemical energy, the only by-products that they release are oxygen and heat. Neither of these by-products is harmful to the environment. Thus, hydrogen fuel cells are pollution-free. However, the challenge lies in developing the technology to harness hydrogen from renewable sources of energy such as solar, wind, and others. Right now, hydrogen, which is used in fuel cell vehicles (FCV), is mostly extracted from fossil fuels.

Mechanism of FCV

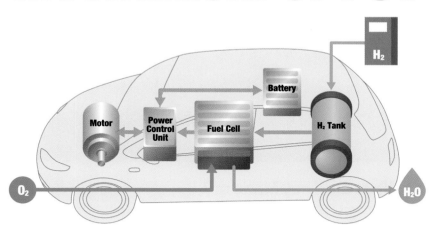

Climate Facts

- The fuel cell was discovered by Christian Friedrich Schönbein in 1838.

- The first fuel cell was built by Welsh scientist Sir William Robert Grove in 1843.

Biofuels

Biofuels are transportation fuels made of biomass (plant or animal material), such as sugarcane, corn, soybeans, algae, and others. They can be mixed with petroleum fuels such as gasoline, or can be used on their own. Biofuels are cleaner-burning fuels as they produce very little air pollutants. However, they are also more expensive than fossil fuels.

What are They Made of?

The terms biofuels and fossil fuels are used interchangeably at times because both are made up of dead and decayed plant or animal matter. The difference between fossil fuels and biofuels is that the latter is made of plants that have recently died, while fossil fuels, like coal, are made of the remains of plants and animals buried deep inside the earth for thousands of years.

Biofuels: Past and Present

Biofuels have been around for a very long time. Wood was the first biofuel used by primitive humans for producing fire and cooking. In fact, biofuels were discovered even before the discovery of fossil fuels. In the 1850s, a biofuel called ethanol was used as a lighting fuel. The use of ethanol increased during the Second World War when oil and other fossil fuel resources became scarce. Presently, ethanol and gasoline are used to run vehicles such as cars and trucks. Ethanol blends are also used to power small engines such as lawn mowers and chainsaws. Experiments are being conducted to develop the technology to use biofuels to power aircrafts.

Climate Facts

• At present, ethanol and biodiesel are the major biofuels in production.

• Rudolf Diesel used peanut oil to run his diesel engine.

Types of Biofuels

thanol and biodiesel are the two main biofuels in use. Currently, biodiesel is mostly made of soybean oil. It can be used directly in place of diesel fuel. Ethanol, on the other hand, is a clear and colorless fuel made of sugars found mainly in corn, barley, and sorghum. Potato skins, sugarcane, and rice can also be used to produce ethanol. Both biodiesel and ethanol are the fastest-growing alternative fuels in the world.

Biodiesel

Biodiesel emits fewer air pollutants. It also has excellent lubricating properties, which make it an ideal transportation fuel. Any vehicle that runs on diesel fuel can easily switch to biodiesel without any change to its engine. The fuel can also be mixed with petroleum diesel. A mixture of 20 percent biodiesel with 80 percent petroleum is called B20. Pure biodiesel and the mixture of biodiesel and petroleum are very sensitive to cold temperatures and must be transported carefully.

Ethanol

Unlike gasoline, pure ethanol is nontoxic. It can be used as a transportation fuel by mixing it with gasoline. A mixture of 10 percent ethanol with 90 percent gasoline (E10) is commonly used. E85 is a fuel that contains about 85 percent ethanol and the vehicles that run on E85 are called Flexible Fuel Vehicles (FFV). Like gasoline, ethanol is extremely flammable and requires special care while transportation.

Reduce Warming

Substituting petroleum fuels with biodiesel or ethanol for transportation can reduce the emission of GHGs from automobiles. Though carbon dioxide and some other gases are released while burning biofuels, their amount is much lower in comparison to emissions released by fossil fuels. An added advantage is that biofuels are renewable since more crops can be grown to produce more biofuels.

 Climate Facts

- When biodiesel burns, it smells like French fries.
- In 2013, 6.9 billion gallons (26.1 billion l) of biodiesel were used in about sixty-five countries.

1. What was the worldwide event in the 1800s that has spurred the rise in global temperatures?

2. Name two of the solar-powered objects mentioned in the text.

3. What is passive solar energy?

4. What is the name for the massive machines that create power using the wind?

5. What is the source of geothermal power?

6. Name two types of marine or ocean energy.

7. Where is the Three Gorges Dam?

8. Name one of the two major types of biofuel.

RESEARCH PROJECTS

1. Pick one area of renewable energy described in the text. Then look further into it, focusing on the United States statistics in that area. Is this type of renewable energy increasing in use? Make a chart about three programs that you find, either national or regional, that are trying to improve this particular area.

2. Research your area's local renewable energy program. What percentage of your local energy comes from renewable sources?

3. Make the case for your family's home to be switched to solar water heating. Compare costs of the panels and installation with water and heating bills. How long will it take to pay off the investment? Make a chart with the pros and cons.

Books

Nardo, Don. *Careers in Renewable Energy.* San Diego: Reference Point Publishing, 2018.

Small, Cathleen. *Wind, Waves, and the Sun.* New York: Cavendish Square, 2018.

Washburne, Sophie. *Alternative Energy Sources: The End of Fossil Fuels?* New York: Lucent Books, 2019.

On the Internet

World Renewable Energy Congress
www.wrenuk.co.uk/

U.S. Energy Information Administration
www.eia.gov/energyexplained/?page=renewable_home

Renewable Energy World
www.renewableenergyworld.com/index.html

bioaccumulation the process of the buildup of toxic chemical substances in the body

biodiversity the diversity of plant and animal life in a habitat (or in the world as a whole)

ecosystem refers to a community of organisms, their interaction with each other, and their physical environment

famine a severe shortage of food (as through crop failure), resulting in hunger, starvation, and death

hydrophobic tending to repel and not absorb water

irrigation the method of providing water to agricultural fields

La Niña periodic, significant cooling of the surface waters of the equatorial Pacific Ocean, which causes abnormal weather patterns

migration the movement of persons or animals from one country or locality to another

pollutants the foreign materials which are harmful to the environment

precipitation the falling to earth of any form of water (rain, snow, hail, sleet, or mist)

stressors processes or events that cause stress

susceptible yielding readily to or capable of

symbiotic the interaction between organisms (especially of different species) that live together and happen to benefit from each other

vulnerable someone or something that can be easily harmed or attacked

INDEX

Photo Credits